G✷D'S
direction is always
BEST®

> *He will be our guide.*
> Psalm 48:14 KJV

DEVOTIONS FOR MEN
TIM WESEMANN

His Message. Your Mission.

The vision of CTA is to see Christians highly effective
in their ministry so that Christ's Kingdom
is strengthened and expanded.

TIM WESEMANN

Copyright © 2018 CTA, Inc.
1625 Larkin Williams Rd.
Fenton, MO 63026
www.CTAinc.com

ISBN 978-1-943216-62-8
PRINTED IN THAILAND

God's Direction
Is Always Best

May the Lord direct your hearts to the love of God
and to the steadfastness of Christ.

2 Thessalonians 3:5

Make me to know your ways, O Lord;
teach me your paths.
Lead me in your truth and teach me,
for you are the God of my salvation;
for you I wait all the day long.

Psalm 25:4–5

Cross-Country Trip!

He will be our guide.
Psalm 48:14 KJV

Anyone up for a cross-country trip?

What? Road trip! Count me in. Load up the car and let's go!

But wait. Reality check.

→ Can we postpone this until things slow down at work?
→ My savings account is nearly empty.
→ I might get carsick.
→ Oops, I should have checked with my wife first.

Don't worry—I'm not talking about leaving the neighborhood, city, or region. Here's the plan for the next five weeks: Jesus has invited us to follow him, so we're going *cross*-country. We'll be taking in the extreme, sacrificial love he has for us and strengthening our faith mile by mile.

Jesus will be our Guide, providing the plan, the means, and the resources we need. The adventure will lead us through homes, gyms, restaurants, cubical mazes, sporting venues, the open road—wherever we travel throughout each day.

Following our Guide will include daily trips to the cross, where Jesus gave his life as the perfect, atoning sacrifice for our sins and our salvation. We'll stop there as our repentant hearts receive his full forgiveness. We'll stand in awe at the resurrection tomb, where he shares the great news of his victorious, never-ending life.

He will take the lead, directing us by his Word and Spirit. No matter what challenges, temptations, and hurts we face in this broken world, he will bring us peace and joy.

Before we set off, be prepared. God may not always lead us along the route we want or plan to travel. Sometimes we may be absolutely oblivious of the itinerary! He may have to repeat his instructions countless times.

But know this: God's direction is always best. He knows all things. He has the entire plan already worked out, and he assures us that *all of it* will work for the good of his people.

Okay, we're all set! We'll be traveling confidently through each day, for "he will be our guide" (Psalm 48:14 KJV).

Trust in the Lord with all your heart,
* and do not lean on your own understanding.*
In all your ways acknowledge him,
* and he will make straight your paths.*

Proverbs 3:5–6

→ **PRAYER STARTER:** Show me your ways, Lord. Direct me down the road of grace that leads to a repentant heart and peace at the foot of your cross . . .

What Route?

*Your word is a lamp to my feet
and a light to my path.*
Psalm 119:105

Most trips offer drivers a variety of routes. Flexible travelers with a sense of adventure can usually make great memories on two-lane highways. Along with impressive scenery, those routes often carry descriptive names like The Road to Nowhere, The Loneliest Road, and The Great River Road.

Since scenic routes usually take longer, I'm guessing travelers often choose a different way home. Saving time seems wise and the thrill of adventure has evaporated.

The alternate route was also the way home for some men known as Magi, who traveled a long way on what could have been named The Starlight Path to Bethlehem. After they worshipped the Christ Child, Jesus, God changed their travel plans:

And being warned in a dream not to return to Herod, [the Wise Men] departed to their own country by another way.
Matthew 2:12

To keep both his own Son and the Magi safe, God directed the Wise Men to take a different route home. To keep them faithful after they got home, he may have put their daily routines on a different route, as well.

After meeting their true Savior, the Magi likely left their reverence for eastern gods by the side of the road in Bethlehem.

Is God nudging you toward an alternate route these days? Perhaps . . .

→ your usual path of selfish pride has led to broken relationships;
→ your preferred route of pet sins is comfortable but taking you away from God's Word; or
→ your win-at-all-costs shortcuts have created outward success at the expense of your faith.

You may look up one day and find yourself lost on a lonely two-lane road to nowhere. But remember, it's not too late to turn around. God has a path of repentance ready and waiting for you. He invites:

Return to the LORD your God, for he is gracious and merciful, slow to anger, and abounding in steadfast love.

Joel 2:13

Best of all, Jesus and his promises of forgiveness and new life follow you wherever you go. Forgiveness frees, lives change, faith grows, and hope triumphs for those who dwell in Jesus' presence.

→ **PRAYER STARTER:** Dear Jesus, change me. Forgive me. Renew my faith. Lead my life down the route you have chosen for me . . .

Planning to Be Spontaneous?

*I will meditate on your precepts and
fix my eyes on your ways.*

Psalm 119:15

A note in my weekly planner says to take a spontaneous trip to visit my son next Friday at 4:00 p.m. Okay, so maybe I'm not the most impulsive guy.

My wife, on the other hand, has no problem deciding a mere day or two in advance to make a ten-hour, multistate trip to see our grandchildren.

Wise decisions often follow meticulous planning as we travel through life as God's faith-filled people. But the wise man Solomon reminds us:

*The heart of man plans his way, but the LORD establishes
his steps.*

Proverbs 16:9

While we make plans, using our God-given discernment and gifts, we also recognize and appreciate that the Lord's wisdom far outweighs our human judgment. We wisely, though sometimes reluctantly, ask the Lord to lead us in his way, even if that takes us in a different direction than we planned.

*Come now, you who say, "Today or tomorrow we will go
into such and such a town and spend a year there and
trade and make a profit"—yet you do not know what
tomorrow will bring. . . . Instead you ought to say, "If the
Lord wills, we will live and do this or that."*

James 4:13–15

We pray that our planning process involves looking to God's will first and our own often-flawed reasoning second. (Or not at all!)

If you're a spur-of-the-moment kind of person, remember this: the Lord can use our faith, compassion, and wisdom in the spontaneous decisions we make throughout each day, too.

He may surprise us with opportunities to show empathy to a struggling co-worker, to pray with a stranger, to listen with heartfelt concern to the needs of a family member, or to gladly forgive, as the Lord has graciously forgiven us.

With Jesus as our travel companion, we set our itinerary. We make plans, trusting at the same time that the Lord will direct us to necessary detours and that the Holy Spirit will surprise us with opportunities for spontaneous acts of grace.

→ **PRAYER STARTER:** Jesus, I love that I can always plan on you to reveal your ways to me and lead me where you want me to go. Teach me to follow with a grateful heart . . .

Making Memories

*Remember your mercy, O LORD, and
your steadfast love, for they have been from of old.*
Psalm 25:6

If you ask people born before 1965 to share some
favorite childhood memories, plenty will share stories
about family vacations. Often, their time spent traveling
together was as memorable as their destination.

Here are a few favorite pre-technology memories some
of you might appreciate:

→ Windows open, no air conditioner, eating PB&J
  sandwiches wrapped in wax paper
→ License plate and alphabet games
→ Getting truckers to blow their horns
→ Photos taken with Polaroid cameras
→ Full-service gas stations with oil checks, window
  washing, and free maps

Granted, not everyone has positive vacation memories.
Arguments, awkward silence, unmet expectations,
frustrations, or bad accidents can make for unhappy
vacation baggage.

In Psalm 77, the writer shares a variety of emotions
tied to his memories. He has his own baggage filled with
complaints, size XL. He cries out to God, wondering if the
Lord is even listening or traveling along with him.

But then, he puts his complaints on hold:

I will remember the deeds of the LORD; yes, I will remember your wonders of old. I will ponder all your work, and meditate on your mighty deeds. Your way, O God, is holy.
Psalm 77:11–13

At this point in his prayer, the psalmist realizes God's direction is best. Have you ever had an a-ha moment like this? You pour out your soul to God and he draws your heart back to his holy heart. Like the psalmist, you can once again see God's goodness, power, and grace, active on your behalf.

Then again, maybe moaning and groaning is the only way you can pray authentically right now. The struggles of life hang like a heavy fog and you can barely see the road right in front of you. Rest assured, God hears those prayers, too. Because of Jesus' sacrifice on the cross, God offers you comfort, no matter how many bad memories you're trying to forget.

I pray that the goodness and grace of our Savior will open your eyes to focus on the good, see the victories, and experience the blessings of traveling with our Lord Jesus.

→ **PRAYER STARTER:** Holy Spirit, help me to recall and give thanks for your unending goodness. What a difference those memories make in my travels through each day . . .

Traveling Companions

*Be strong and courageous. Do not
be frightened, and do not be dismayed,
for the LORD your God is with you wherever you go.*
Joshua 1:9

Jesus walked an estimated 3,000 miles during his three-year public ministry. (I'm not sure if that includes his walks on water.) He walked most of those miles with company, usually his disciples.

Jesus had a special relationship with the twelve men he specifically called to follow him. The disciples had a deep desire to follow Jesus and learn from him—in essence, they wanted to *know* him. They spent lots of time with Jesus, including many hours and miles traveling the dusty roads.

Do you ever wish you could walk with Jesus just like those first disciples? To hear his preaching, experience his miracles, and pray alongside the Savior of the world?

But if you were walking beside him, he'd see all of your faults, wouldn't he?

→ The greed in your heart that holds back your
   giving spirit
→ The addiction that rears its ugly head when no one
   is watching
→ The angry shutdown mode you turn on when you just
   don't want to deal with your family struggles

Jesus saw the shortcomings of his disciples, too—plenty of them! At times his disciples argued, didn't listen, acted like children in front of children, and got upset when they should instead have shown compassion.

But there were also incredible moments of teaching and learning, healing, and prayer. Jesus' mercy and forgiveness were real for those disciples, and they are just as real for you today!

Jesus never fired his disciples, and he'll never let you go, either. Instead, he frees you from the chains of sin. You can take comfort in the same promise he gave to his disciples:

I am with you always, to the end of the age.

Matthew 28:20

Ultimately, we never travel alone—around the house or around the world, on good days or bad days. Our Savior is present. His never-ending forgiveness is here. Always and everywhere.

Enjoy spending time with him . . . hour by hour, mile after mile.

✈ **PRAYER STARTER:** Jesus, I yearn to walk with you just like your first disciples. Strengthen my faith. Show me your grace and use your Word to guide me . . .

Stories from the Road

Consider reading the following memorable travel stories. Each focuses on someone who encountered Jesus while traveling.

→ Luke 24:13–35 documents Jesus, shortly after his resurrection, traveling with two unassuming men on a road that led to Emmaus.

→ Acts 9:1–22 tells the story of one of history's most amazing life changes. It happened in the life of a man named Saul (whose name would later be changed to Paul) after an encounter with Jesus on the road to Damascus.

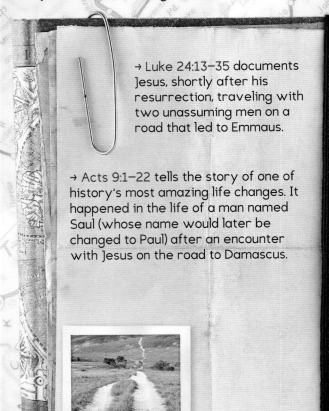

ROAD TRIP CHECKLISTS

I will extol you, my God and King,
and bless your name forever and ever.
Every day I will bless you
and praise your name forever and ever.
Great is the LORD, and greatly to be praised,
and his greatness is unsearchable.
One generation shall commend
your works to another,
and shall declare your mighty acts. . . .
The LORD is righteous in all his ways
and kind in all his works.

Psalm 145:1–4, 17

Checklist #1: Necessities

For I decided to know nothing among you
except Jesus Christ and him crucified.
1 Corinthians 2:2

When planning a road trip, you're likely going to make some lists—in your mind or on a piece of paper. The most important and obvious checklist pertains to basic necessities. Do you have enough money, a clear schedule, and a reliable vehicle?

Many of us write checklists to organize our daily lives, too. For instance . . .

→ Make dentist appointment
→ Buy sports drink for Jimmy's soccer team
→ Help Dad move refrigerator

Sound familiar? The necessities of everyday life can feel boring, like drudgery. Has your list ever looked like this?

→ Make a 2 a.m. run to the drugstore because the kids need cough syrup
→ Forgo a Sunday afternoon of football because the in-laws need help painting
→ Teach your wife how to operate the home security system—for the 50th time!

It's easy to get fed up with life's necessary chores, but

that's only when you forget who's in charge of the checklist:

My God will supply every need . . . according to his riches in glory in Christ Jesus.

Philippians 4:19

In Jesus and in him alone, God provides everything you need. In fact, Jesus himself is *the* list! Saves you from sin—check. Loves you even when you don't deserve it—check. Invites you to eternal life with him—check.

When you entrust your checklist to God, you see it through the lens of the cross and the drudgery disappears. Cleaning up after a sick kid? Jesus has been there—he washed *feet*. Have to help the in-laws again? God grants you patience as you deal with all their requests. Your wife getting on your last nerve? Jesus offers you unlimited forgiveness and that makes it possible for you to forgive her one million times over.

You see, no matter what's on your checklist, God is at work in all of it. He's working through your words and actions to show the true Light of his love to this world. Even the most mundane tasks might just be God's way of leading others to faith in Jesus.

→ **PRAYER STARTER:** Heavenly Father, you're all I need. Remind me that you meet all my needs in Christ crucified . . .

Checklist #2: Contacts

I will offer to you the sacrifice of thanksgiving
and call on the name of the LORD
Psalm 116:17

Technology has made keeping track of our contacts easy. Smartphones, tablets, and laptops make it possible to take our contact list along with us wherever we go. What a blessing when we need help in a travel emergency.

Here's another amazing blessing: the blessing of calling on the name of the Lord in prayer . . . wherever and whenever. We have 24/7 access to the Creator of the universe. From the North Pole to the South Pole, we can talk to the King of kings. The one true triune God is always listening. It's an amazing blessing, really, but one we easily take for granted.

We have a contact list like no other—a Friend in the highest of places. To remind me to call on the Lord first, always, and often, I have added "Jesus Christ" to my smartphone's contact list. He's right at the top of my "favorites" list.

Sounds strange, I know. But it really is a great reminder to spend my time talking to him and not just the others on my list.

It's easy to get distracted by the craziness of our lives. We call our wives, check in at work, and order takeout, but we forget to call upon the One who gave us life. Real life. God's forever kind of life!

Throughout Jesus' life here on earth, he made prayer a priority:

→ *And after he had dismissed the crowds, he went up on the mountain by himself to pray. When evening came, he was there alone.*

Matthew 14:23

→ *[Jesus] went out to the mountain to pray, and all night he continued in prayer to God.*

Luke 6:12

→ *[Jesus] would withdraw to desolate places and pray.*

Luke 5:16

If we went to those mountains and desolate places to pray, it's possible we wouldn't have phone service or Wi-Fi. Maybe that's not such a bad idea. Today, find a quiet place to call on the name of the Lord in prayer, cast your cares on him, and enjoy the peace he brings to your heart.

→ **PRAYER STARTER:** Dear Jesus, I know you're always there to listen. Hear my prayer . . .

Checklist #3: Packing

I will greatly rejoice in the LORD; my soul shall exult in my God, for he has clothed me with the garments of salvation.

Isaiah 61:10

Most men find packing for road trips pretty easy. We usually go with the bare minimum. Shirts. Check. Pants or shorts. Check. Socks. Check. Underwear. Check. Shoes. Check. Check. Total time: 7 minutes, 20 seconds.

Anything I missed?

Granted, there's the bathroom stuff and tech gadgets, but I'm thinking more about suitcase packing—what we'll be wearing. What would you add to your packing checklist?

The apostle Paul created a similar checklist—spiritually speaking. His list includes the things we are to put on day by day. These things will affect our own lives and the lives of those around us:

Put on then, as God's chosen ones, holy and beloved, compassionate hearts, kindness, humility, meekness, and patience, bearing with one another and, if one has a complaint against another, forgiving each other; as the Lord has forgiven you, so you also must forgive. And above all these put on love, which binds everything together in perfect harmony. And let the peace of Christ rule in your hearts.

Colossians 3:12–15

All that seems like much more than one suitcase—or one heart—can hold! What do you think? Can your heart hold all of this? Or does it lose these qualities as easily as some airlines lose luggage?

Before you answer, imagine the morning when your broken coffeemaker ends up in the trash, along with your last shred of patience. Your kindness flies out the window as your non-caffeinated mind flips into road-rage mode. Then, forgiveness evaporates when your co-worker throws you under the bus with a big-name client.

Even if you haven't had a day exactly like this, you know, deep down, that the items on Paul's packing checklist are too much for us to handle.

But we need not rely on ourselves! We can turn to the Holy Spirit. He reminds us of our Savior's death for all our failures. He covers us with Jesus' righteousness.

As God's chosen, forgiven sons, we are able to latch that overfilled suitcase and bring the peace of Christ along with us—wherever our travels may take us.

→ **PRAYER STARTER:** Holy Spirit, teach me to travel with gratitude for all your gifts . . .

Checklist #4: Snacks

How sweet are your words to my taste,
sweeter than honey to my mouth!
Psalm 119:103

I can't imagine a road trip without snacks. When traveling, I add miles to my odometer and pounds to my body. My snack list includes foods that are salty, an excessive variety of sweets, a few healthy snacks (if my wife is along), and keep-me-awake caffeine drinks.

What's on your top-ten checklist of road trip snacks?

Today's Bible verse describes God's Word as sweet, sweeter than honey. It satisfies us and keeps us moving forward. One taste and you want more. God's Word is healthy—physically, mentally, and spiritually.

It goes well with traveling, too. Two verses later the psalmist writes:

Your word is a lamp to my feet and a light to my path.
Psalm 119:105

When do you crave God's sweet, faith-strengthening nourishment? Consider memorizing the tasty morsels below. They'll keep you moving forward as you navigate through life.

When sin leads you down a dark road:

God is our refuge and strength, a very present help in trouble.

Psalm 46:1

When your life starts to lose focus:

[Jesus said,] "I am the way, and the truth, and the life. No one comes to the Father except through me."

John 14:6

When it seems you can't do anything right:

For the wages of sin is death, but the free gift of God is eternal life in Christ Jesus our Lord.

Romans 6:23

When you're tempted to give in to the ways of the world:

I have been crucified with Christ. It is no longer I who live, but Christ who lives in me.

Galatians 2:20

When you don't measure up to expectations at work or at home:

My grace is sufficient for you, for my power is made perfect in weakness.

2 Corinthians 12:9

As you call upon the Word of God, your body and soul will thank you. Unlike calorie-laden road trip snacks, God's Word truly nourishes your heart. It creates peace, forgiveness, and joy. Plus, you don't have to worry about a sugar crash—just open up your Bible to receive its benefits all over again.

→ **PRAYER STARTER:** Heavenly Father, create in me a deep craving for your nourishing, life-sustaining words of life. Give me great joy in sharing them with others . . .

Checklist #5: Maintenance

You [O, Lord] ... are acquainted with all my ways.
Psalm 139:3

When I was young and my dad's side of the family got together, the men would gather outside around one of their cars. My uncles raised the hood and would discuss every detail of the car. They knew cars inside and out.

I can imagine the extreme care they took in getting their cars ready for a road trip. They undoubtedly wanted everything to be perfect.

Perfection was God's plan too. And it was achieved ... in the beginning. Then, with a fury, Satan rolled into the Garden of Eden like a viper in the first hybrid model of temptation and sin. Adam and Eve lost their focus on their Creator. They sinned against their God, who then drove them out of the Garden. Sin changed everything.

The world was broken. Perfection ended. Humankind could've been headed for the junkyard, but God never abandoned Adam and Eve. Instead, he promised to send a Savior, one who would overpower their sin—Jesus Christ.

As the Holy Spirit creates faith through God's Word, he directs us to the cross of Jesus. Like a mechanic that keeps a 1957 Chevy running, Jesus makes us new every morning. Forgiven in the cross, we stand shining in the Son. The Father sees his Son's perfection in us.

When we stumble and our sins seem too much to bear, we return to the foot of the cross. There, we're reminded that Christ promises to live in us and through us:

I have been crucified with Christ. It is no longer I who live, but Christ who lives in me. And the life I now live in the flesh I live by faith in the Son of God, who loved me and gave himself for me.

Galatians 2:20

The total perfection, ruined in Eden, will be fully restored in the New Heavens and New Earth that God promises (2 Peter 3:13). Until then, we live confident in the promises of our Savior.

So each day, remember to fill up on forgiveness, always consult divine directions, and buckle up for a blessed ride!

→ **PRAYER STARTER:** Father, I ask for your forgiveness and give thanks for the promises I have in my Savior. Lead me in the way of the cross, for your direction is always best . . .

Stories from the Road: Part 2

In Psalm 18, David presents a poetic prayer to God. Study his prayer and note the checklist of things for which he asks:

→ Confidence in the ways of the Lord
→ Praise for the ever-present help of the Lord
→ Thanksgiving for God's rescue
→ Praise for the almighty strength of God
→ Worship of the Lord's holiness
→ Joy in the living Lord

Do your prayers mirror David's psalm? If you struggle to find the words to pray, grab a note card and write down ten things to pray about: family members, friends who don't know Jesus, thanksgiving to God for your blessings, and so on. Carry that note card in your wallet and get it out anytime you want to talk to your heavenly Father. Next week, get a new note card and write a fresh checklist.

Navigating through Your Days

Trust in the Lord with all your heart, and do not lean on your own understanding. In all your ways acknowledge him, and he will make straight your paths.

Proverbs 3:5–6

The Lord is my shepherd; I shall not want.
He makes me lie down in green pastures.
He leads me beside still waters.
He restores my soul.
He leads me in paths of righteousness for his name's sake.

Psalm 23:1–3

Navigation System vs. Map

Commit your way to the Lord; trust in him, and he will act.
Psalm 37:5

I want to trust navigation systems; I really do. But instead, I have a love-hate relationship with them. They impress me, but I can't bring myself to trust them 100 percent. There are too many unknowns.

If I'm going on a long trip, I often print a map—just in case my navigation system fails. Then I confidently turn on my car and take off, backup plan in hand.

Can we be confident *without* a backup plan?
Abraham was:

By faith Abraham obeyed when he was called to go out to a place that he was to receive as an inheritance. And he went out, not knowing where he was going.
Hebrews 11:8

No navigation system. No map. Just trust in God. Seriously, Abraham? Seriously!

When the Lord spoke, Abraham listened. He and his family trusted God 100 percent. They followed the Lord's direction and plan, leaving their country and extended family.

Who has that kind of trust? When you're down to the last $50 in your bank account . . . when your friend is diagnosed with cancer . . . when your co-workers dismiss your faith as quackery—can you trust that God's direction is always best?

The full-fledged trust that Abraham displayed is possible only for the righteous—those who know and trust the righteousness Christ gives and who rely on the forgiveness he won for us.

There is no backup plan for our salvation. We can trust God's flawless navigation, the navigation that took Jesus from a stable in Bethlehem to a cross at Golgotha to an empty tomb on Easter morning. Jesus is our Savior, and he'll never let us down.

We don't need a map because God tells us where to go. Dead in our sins, we look to Jesus to make us alive. Unsure of where to turn next, we focus our eyes on the cross. Walking as strangers here on earth, we place our hope in Jesus and the mansion he's preparing in heaven.

Put your trust in the divine Navigator, Jesus Christ. When you feel yourself reaching for a backup plan, pray! Ask for God's direction, trust his forgiveness, and always keep the cross in sight.

→ **PRAYER STARTER:** Lord God, I can't see the future, but I know you are leading me . . .

Navigation System Fail

*Blessed is the one whose transgression
is forgiven, whose sin is covered.*

Psalm 32:1

A few years ago, my wife and I were on the road after visiting our grandkids in a different state. Eager to get home, we decided to take a shortcut recommended by our GPS. It was an utter disaster. Slow two-lane highways and construction messes everywhere! It didn't take us long to recognize this was an epic GPS *fail*.

You've heard of Cain, Noah, and David, right? Their stories, and countless others in the Bible, are full of epic fails. In fact, sin, depravity, and failure is part of life for every person who walks the earth:

→ Cain murdered his brother (Genesis 4:1–16).
→ Noah planted a vineyard and got drunk (Genesis 9:20–21).
→ David tried to conceal his adultery with murder
   (2 Samuel 11).
→ You yourself act at times as if you worship money
   (Exodus 32).
→ You're sometimes ruled by sexual temptations
   (1 Kings 11:1–8).
→ Your heart is often full of jealousy and anger
   (1 Samuel 18:6–16).

The story of God's people—then and now—is a story that includes much rebellion and sin. What a huge mess! The only way out is **G**od's **P**lan of **S**alvation (GPS, if you will).

There are no shortcuts in God's plan. Instead of justifiably destroying us and all sinners, he chose one person to serve as the object of all his wrath. That One was Jesus. Born of a woman, true flesh and blood, he lived a perfect human life in our place. He fulfilled the Law because we couldn't.

Jesus went to the cross to take the wrath we had earned, to be the sacrifice for our sins. But what looked like an epic fail became a true and amazing victory when Jesus rose from the dead. Through faith, Jesus' new life has become our own. Our sins created the mess, but he cleaned it up with his blood.

No matter the shortcuts you've taken, the sins you've committed, or the epic failures you've lived, Jesus offers the hope of Good News. He gave his life for your sins. No one deserves that kind of love and forgiveness, and there's nothing you can do to earn it. It's a gift. It's yours. Full forgiveness. Real peace. Epic grace.

→ **PRAYER STARTER:** Jesus, you gave your life to save me. You took the punishment I deserve . . .

GPS Message: Recalculating

There is joy before the angels of God over one sinner who repents.

Luke 15:10

Beginning in 2011, many GPS manufacturers decided to do away with the "recalculating" message. It seems the companies received too many complaints about the GPS voice calling out the driver's mistakes—er, I mean "alternate routes."

Drivers sent in comments like these:

→ I know I missed the exit. And then my GPS announces "recalculating!" Don't rub it in and give my family reason to get upset with me. We all know I messed up!

→ I went off course on purpose to get something to eat. I knew what I was doing. Stop telling me I was wrong!

→ I'm tired of constantly hearing "recalculating!" It's too much, too often. I'm hearing it in my sleep!

When we veer from God's direction, we don't like being reminded of it, either. Sometimes we deliberately disobey. We know we're headed along the wrong route, but we continue anyway. Other times, we don't do it intentionally. It just happens.

Our sinful decisions come so rapidly and often, we're tired of hearing about them. But we do need to hear about them. We do need to recalculate. In love, our Lord will always encourage us to rethink our decisions when we're headed off course.

David certainly heard that message. In Psalm 32, he recounts feeling the Lord's heavy hand on him, the weight of guilt. God reminded David again and again to recalculate. Then, when David did turn to the Lord and away from his sin, the Lord forgave him and restored the joy of his salvation.

We may not always like being reminded of our sin, but God loves us too much to stop. As we grow in that gracious truth, we find that we want him to shed light on our sin because it points us to Jesus. The forgiveness he earned on the cross is always ours, no matter how much "recalculating" is necessary.

As we set our path, our joy comes in following God's ways, will, and direction—which are always best.

→ **PRAYER STARTER:** Dear God, in the midst of my sins, the Holy Spirit has brought me to repentance. In Jesus' name, forgive me for . . .

SLOW DOWN

GPS Message: Make a U-Turn

If we are faithless, he remains faithful—for he cannot deny himself.
2 Timothy 2:13

Imagine a complicated strip-mall parking lot on a Saturday afternoon. There are cars everywhere. The "to the highway" signs seem to point in different directions. To add to the chaos, your GPS keeps repeating the same message: "Make a U-turn when possible."

Life can be a lot like that crowded, complicated parking lot. Temptations are everywhere—at home, at work, even at church! We turn away from God's will, ways, and laws. Then, when we make a self-chosen U-turn, trying to get back on the right route, we end up more confused than before.

That's because the "U-turn" message isn't exactly correct. It gives the impression that we do the turning, putting ourselves back on God's path of righteousness. In reality, the Christ-follower's prayer should be "*You-turn me, Holy Spirit.*"

The prophet Elijah took this "you-turn me" message to the Israelites at Mount Carmel. He knew they had turned away from the one true God and were worshipping the idol-god Baal. Gathering all the prophets of Baal together, Elijah called on the living and active Lord, Yahweh, to show his presence and power while exposing Baal as counterfeit. Elijah prayed:

*Answer me, O Lord, answer me, that this people may know that you, O Lord, are God, **and that you have turned their hearts back.***

1 Kings 18:37, emphasis added

Elijah knew the people weren't going to turn back to God on their own. The same is true for us. When we rely on our own ways, our own wisdom, and our own "spirituality," we end up going nowhere, lost, endlessly turning around in circles. The only thing that can stop the cycle of sin is the Holy Spirit working repentance in our hearts.

When you're in a mess of sin and feeling disoriented, consider this:

Don't you see how wonderfully kind, tolerant, and patient God is with you? Does this mean nothing to you? Can't you see that his kindness is intended to turn you from your sin?

Romans 2:4 NLT

God graciously gives us the gift of repentance. Follow his way and gladly ask, "You-turn me, Lord God, to my ever-present Redeemer, Jesus!"

→ **PRAYER STARTER:** Direct all of my ways, Lord, so that . . .

GPS Message: Lost Signal

*When he calls to me, I will answer him; I will be
with him in trouble; I will rescue him and honor him.*
Psalm 91:15

It's your worst nightmare: While driving in an unfamiliar
city, the dreaded "Lost Signal" message appears on your
navigation system. The GPS signal is lost and so are you.

We men don't like admitting we're lost. It kills our
confidence and forces us to accept defeat. Instead of
reaching out for help, we have an internal debate about
how to get back on track:

*Did I miss a turn five miles back or was it 25 miles? What
about my schedule? I can't be lost now—we have to get
home! I'm going to charge ahead.*

It's tough admitting that you've lost your way—and that
applies to more than just road trips. We can feel so lost
when we've been blindsided by unemployment. Or when
relationships with family members are contentious. Or
when we're stuck in a rut and seem to be okay with it.
Life is often one struggle after another and there are no
rest stops in sight.

A paralyzed man in Capernaum
could likely relate to our
feelings of lostness. Scripture
doesn't say, but he likely spent
days (maybe months and
years) lost in his thoughts of
despair. He probably believed
his future went no further than

his cot. But one day, things started looking up as four men lowered him down from a roof into the presence of Jesus (Mark 2:1–12).

Jesus was preaching the Word in a home and the place was standing room (and one cot) only. Seeing the faith of the paralyzed man's friends, Jesus addressed the most important issue in the man's life. Jesus forgave his sins. Miracle one.

And then, after Jesus addressed the bullying objections of his own enemies, religious leaders lost in the law, Jesus healed the man. Miracle two.

Both miracles gave the man a leg to stand on as he walked by faith toward his future. If you find yourself lost in sickness, anxiety, or guilt, remember Jesus' words:

For the Son of Man came to seek and to save the lost.

Luke 19:10

Jesus will seek you. He will save you. The miraculous sin-forgiving, life-giving, lost-finder Jesus is yours—today and always!

→ **PRAYER STARTER:** Jesus, I need your miracles of forgiveness and healing in so many ways . . .

Stories from the Road: Part 3

Use the Images link of an Internet search to look up "travel route to the Promised Land." The results will show you the route Moses took while leading God's people from captivity in Egypt to the Promised Land of Canaan.

Once you see the map, you'll understand why those 40 years are often described as "wandering" in the wilderness. There were plenty of U-turns, recalculations, and lost signals!

The Lord used those years of traveling to teach his people to trust him in all areas of their lives and to recognize him as the one true God.

What has the Lord taught you about trusting him and acknowledging him as the one true God—Father, Son, and Holy Spirit—while you have been traveling through each day of your life?

PLACES OF INTEREST

*I will extol you, my God and King,
and bless your name forever and ever.
Every day I will bless you
and praise your name forever and ever.
Great is the L*ORD*, and greatly to be praised,
and his greatness is unsearchable.
One generation shall commend your
works to another,
and shall declare your mighty acts.*

Psalm 145:1–4

The Grand Canyon

The earth is the LORD's and the fullness thereof,
the world and those who dwell therein.

Psalm 24:1

If you were planning a road trip to visit the most inspiring, magnificent spots in God's creation, where would you go? Maybe you'd want to take in the giant sequoias of Yosemite or the geysers of Yellowstone. You might visit Niagara Falls or Mount Rainier. Perhaps you'd stop to see an ocean, a volcano, or a glacier.

For me, the Grand Canyon is at the top of the list. I've been there a few times, and I still haven't found a way to describe its grandeur. Its size—277 miles long, 6,000 feet deep, 5.45 trillion cubic yards of volume—is simply spectacular!

And yet, I know an even bigger canyon. It's the expanse that separates us from our heavenly Father and the gift of heaven. Our sins have created an immeasurable divide:

But your iniquities have made a separation
between you and your God,
and your sins have hidden his face from you
so that he does not hear.

Isaiah 59:2

Geologists say the Grand Canyon is constantly getting deeper and wider. The same thing happens when we try to earn salvation. It only creates a wider gulf. When we try to impress God with our own holiness, the valleys in our heart only grow deeper.

Because we are dead in our sins, relying on our own abilities and good works to bridge the gap is futile! There is only one way out of the canyon and it's Jesus.

We receive forgiveness and eternal life in Jesus Christ, and in him alone. His sacrificial death on the cross and resurrection victory three days later have made us friends of God—forever!

The bridge-building, salvation-giving, sin-forgiving Son of God, Jesus Christ, told the world:

I am the way, and the truth, and the life. No one comes to the Father except through me.

John 14:6

So don't even think about relying on yourself to build a bridge across the cavernous gap of sin! Jesus' work on the cross built the bridge, and God graciously invites you to cross it. Go ahead—take in the wonder of it all and run home to your Father.

→ **PRAYER STARTER:** Jesus, I can hardly describe how thankful I am that your grace has bridged the gap my sinful life created . . .

Roadside Attractions

For the word of the cross is folly to those who are perishing,
but to us who are being saved it is the power of God.
1 Corinthians 1:18

Roadside attractions usually aren't destinations. They're simply stopping places along the way to the destination. I'm thinking about one-of-a-kind, larger-than-life oddities like the world's largest golf tee, knitting needles, and catsup bottle.

As Jesus and his disciples traveled, Jesus himself often became a roadside attraction, as it were. People had heard about his teachings and miracles. They wanted to know more. Was he the world's greatest teacher or largest fraud? one-of-a-kind miracle worker or a roadside sideshow? Was he sent by God or just playing god?

The people who met Jesus in the midst of his travels quickly learned he was much more than a roadside attraction. Meeting the Son of God changed their daily lives and eternal destinations:

→ Two blind men cried out to Jesus for healing. He touched their eyes and gave them sight. Their response? They followed him. (See Matthew 20:29–34.)
→ Traversing a mountain road, people with all kinds of infirmities went to see Jesus. He healed them all and Scripture tells us the crowd glorified the God of Israel. (See Matthew 15:29–31.)
→ During his ministry, Jesus healed the minds and bodies of several women. They responded in gratitude by helping and serving Jesus and his disciples. (See Luke 8:1–3.)

→ After witnessing Jesus' crucifixion, death, and the aftermath, a Roman centurion ultimately recognized him as the Son of God. (See Matthew 27:54.)

Jesus wasn't a roadside attraction—he was (and still is!) *the* destination. Yes, his gifts are larger than life. Perhaps they seem unbelievable at times. But you don't want to make the mistake of driving on by, looking for a fancier destination! Go directly to him for healing, mercy, and forgiveness. He will welcome you with unconditional love and the promise of eternal life.

By living in Jesus, we find the strength to model our lives after his ministry—taking time to care for others, responding to their needs, teaching them eternal truths. Jesus served generously and he calls us to do the same.

→ **PRAYER STARTER:** Jesus, I am beyond grateful that you saw me on the road to hell and changed my eternal destination . . .

Amusement Parks

A joyful heart is good medicine, but a
crushed spirit dries up the bones.
Proverbs 17:22

For roller-coaster fanatics, Kingda Ka reigns supreme.
The ride launches passengers 45 stories into the air and
reaches a top speed of 128 miles per hour. What a thrill!

Even if you don't like roller coasters, amusement parks
are a great vacation destination. You'll find bumper cars,
Ferris wheels, water rides, carnival food, and lots of other
treats designed to bring joy and laughter to your family.

As God's people were returning home to Israel after
70 years of exile in Babylon, they felt exhilaration, joy,
giddiness, and every other happy emotion you can
imagine. They laughed as their longed-for dreams
came true.

They knew the Lord had made their return possible and
they were thankful. You can sense their excitement and
gratitude in the words of the psalmist:

When the Lord restored the fortunes of Zion,
  we were like those who dream.
Then our mouth was filled with laughter,
  and our tongue with shouts of joy;
then they said among the nations,
  "The Lord has done great things for them."
The Lord has done great things for us;
  we are glad.

Psalm 126:1–3

A dream! God had given his people so many blessings that they thought they were dreaming. No grumbling, no weeping. Joy! Laughter! It was like an amusement park vacation that never had to end!

How do you feel these days? As exuberant as God's people returning to Jerusalem? Like a miserable schmuck stuck inside a whack-a-mole arcade game? Or like you're riding the highs and lows of a roller coaster?

No matter what ride you're on, your Savior promises to be with you in it all. In your joy, he rejoices with you and hears your prayers of thanksgiving. When you're hurting, he knows your pain and he cries with you. In times of uncertainty, he stands strong as your rock and fortress.

Because of Jesus, you can rejoice in the blessings of the Lord no matter what life throws at you. Sing out with all the people of God: "The Lord has done great things for us and we're thankful!"

→ **PRAYER STARTER:** God, you are so good to me! Teach me to see the blessings and feel the joy of Jesus in every situation . . .

From Oceans to Deserts

For your steadfast love is before my eyes,
and I walk in your faithfulness.
Psalm 26:3

When traveling coast to coast across the United States, you can't help but notice drastic changes in the landscape. The deserts of Nevada, the mountains of Colorado, the prairies of Kansas, the woodlands of Vermont—all point to the creativity of our Creator.

As we move through life, we may also encounter drastic changes. We may reach the mountaintops of life with a strong, energized faith. Then, our faith may fall, feeling sea-level low and desert dry. Our faith may seem as consistent as the ocean's tides or as desolate as a tumbleweed blowing across the prairie.

David, who encountered incredible highs and painful lows in his life of faith, is always raw, open, and honest in his psalms and prayers.

Consider a few of his words:

O God, you are my God; earnestly I seek you; my soul thirsts for you; my flesh faints for you, as in a dry and weary land where there is no water.

Psalm 63:.

Consider and answer me, O LORD my God; light up my eyes, lest I sleep the sleep of death.

Psalm 13:.

Every day I will bless you and praise your name forever and ever.

Psalm 145:2

If you're struggling with what seems like a radically inconsistent faith, remember this: God's love for you isn't based on the strength of your faith. Your heavenly Father sent Jesus to live a perfect life of faith for you, to show unwavering obedience to God, and to follow through on the promise to be your Savior.

Did he do this because you *deserve* it, because your faith *earned* it? No! He did it fully knowing that you're a sinner!

So when you find your faith trapped in Death Valley, rest assured that the Holy Spirit created your faith. He promises to work through God's Word, with God's people, and during times of worship to strengthen your faith.

Focus not on yourself but on the unwavering, perfect love of Jesus Christ. You can find confidence knowing that you are forgiven and covered in his righteousness. Whether you're reaching the summit or walking the flat land, you are always traveling with a Spirit-created, life-saving faith.

→ **PRAYER STARTER:** Jesus, be near me on the mountaintops and in the valleys. Lead me to . . .

Unplanned Stops

*When he went ashore he saw a great crowd,
and he had compassion on them, because they
were like sheep without a shepherd.*

Mark 6:34

No road trip is complete without a few impromptu stops.
"World's Best Ice Cream" shop. Flat tire. Scenic overlook.
Turtle family crossing the road. Motion sickness.

There are two kinds of unplanned travel stops: *good*
and *not so good.* Usually, it's easy to categorize each
situation. But, sometimes what you'd expect to see in
the *not so good* column surprises you and turns into a
positive pit stop.

The apostle Paul spent a lot of time traveling on the road
and on the water. Paul's journey as a servant for Christ
started with a very unexpected stop along the road to
Damascus. Jesus interrupted Paul's trip to miraculously
change his heart and his mission. Paul went from someone
who persecuted Christ's followers to someone who was
persecuted for his faith in Christ.

Here is a portion of Paul's travel log:

*Three times I was beaten with rods. Once I was stoned.
Three times I was shipwrecked; a night and a day I was
adrift at sea; on frequent journeys, in danger from rivers,
danger from robbers, . . . through many a sleepless night, in
hunger and thirst, often without food, in cold and exposure.*

2 Corinthians 11:25–27

How would you like to travel with him? A flat tire doesn't seem so bad now, does it?

Even amidst his unexpected stops, plenty of them in the *not so good* category, Paul continuously encouraged God's people by reminding them:

We know that for those who love God all things work together for good, for those who are called according to his purpose.

Romans 8:28

You can plan on your Savior having plans for your unplanned situations. He may unexpectedly call on you to encourage a struggling co-worker. He may put an unplanned stop in your family life so that you'll be able to serve your community. He may be working good for you, even though you're struggling to survive an illness.

Embrace the unplanned stops! Jesus Christ is present in every one of them, working for you and through you, for the glory of God.

→ **PRAYER STARTER:** Gracious God, lead me. Your direction is always best. Show me where to stop and teach me to expect the unexpected . . .

Stories from the Road: Part 4

A long road trip gives you time to talk to your fellow passengers. You might indulge in surface chat, start a deep conversation, or share a few laughs.

On the other hand, when conversations get a little tense or heated, you can't just open the vehicle's door and walk out. Travel companions are basically stuck together. People shut down. There's awkward silence and increasing frustration.

Is there someone you're "stuck" with today? Are you traveling with atheistic co-workers, rude neighbors, or ungrateful children?

Take a few moments to consider what God is teaching you in this situation. What does God want you to see? Is he telling you to change your route, slow down, or speed on to your destination? Could this be an opportunity for Christian witness or compassion?

LEARNING FROM OUR GUIDE

Therefore, since we are surrounded by so great a cloud of witnesses, let us also lay aside every weight, and sin which clings so closely, and let us run with endurance the race that is set before us, looking to Jesus, the founder and perfecter of our faith, who for the joy that was set before him endured the cross, despising the shame, and is seated at the right hand of the throne of God. Consider him who endured from sinners such hostility against himself, so that you may not grow weary or fainthearted.

Hebrews 12:1–3

Rest Areas

So God blessed the seventh day and made it holy, because on it God rested from all his work that he had done in creation.

Genesis 2:3

Seasoned travelers love the simplicity of rest areas. These stops don't have the same distractions as regular exits. There is one bathroom, one vending machine, and one area for the dog to take a break.

Unfortunately, it seems like rest stops are never there when you need them. The same can often be said of us—we're speeding down the highway of life with nowhere to stop for rest.

In today's Bible verse, we see God creating the Sabbath day. In Hebrew, *Sabbath* means "day of rest." God's Old Testament people observed Saturday as the Sabbath day. Now, we celebrate the Sabbath on Sunday to commemorate the resurrection of Jesus.

God set aside Sunday for rest and worship, but when we move a million miles per hour through the rest of the week, one day of rest is simply not enough. Our Father knows us intimately—he created us. He knows our need for *daily* rest and meditation in his Word.

It's difficult to stop and rest, I know. Instead of pulling off the highway at a simple rest area, we turn toward the exit for the big city. So much to see, so many places to go. Distractions everywhere! One big headache!

Have you felt this? A complicated commute means you have to leave home early and miss your morning devotions. You sit down to rest in the evening but feel compelled to keep checking your smartphone. Your thoughts and worries keep you up at night. Then, you spend the next day even more sleep-deprived and unfocused than before.

You can't rest, on Sunday or any other day, until you entrust your cares to your heavenly Father, finding your rest in him:

*Be still before the L*ORD *and wait patiently for him.*

Psalm 37:7

In your stillness, the Lord will calm your fears and silence your distractions. He will give you wisdom and guidance. You'll feel the grace and mercy of Jesus flowing into your life.

Take a break, relax, unplug from work, and tune out the world. Jesus has a rest stop waiting for you and it gets perfect reviews.

→ **PRAYER STARTER:** Jesus, help me to see and seize the opportunities you give me for rest . . .

I'm Hungry!

The eyes of all look to you, and you give them their food in due season. You open your hand; you satisfy the desire of every living thing.
Psalm 145:15–16

I love eating out when I'm on the road. I especially gravitate toward local fare—Cincinnati caviar, Hoppin' John, Maid Rites. Yum, yum, yum!

Even though you and I can find all types of restaurants on the road, that wasn't the case in Jesus' time. In particular, Jesus and his disciples once faced a crowd of 5,000 hungry people on the shore of the Sea of Galilee.

Jesus had spent the day healing and teaching. It was getting late and the disciples were getting worried. This was a big crowd, it was almost suppertime, and they were in the middle of nowhere. So, the disciples encouraged Jesus to send the people on their way to get something to eat.

Jesus gives what seems to be a nonchalant response:

You give them something to eat.

Matthew 14:16

I would love to have seen their faces at that point. The disciples were shocked. They didn't have the resources to feed a crowd that big!

But Jesus already had it figured out. With the power of the Son of God, two fish and five loaves of bread would be plenty. He wasn't concerned.

The twelve disciples, however, *were* a concern. They weren't thinking like disciples of their Rabbi. They were blind to the power of Jesus. Had they forgotten his miracles? Couldn't they see who Jesus was?

The disciples were quick to doubt Jesus. Their human minds couldn't comprehend such a simple solution to such a big problem. But that's who Jesus is—human flesh like me and you, born in a simple stable, but also the Son of God on a mission to rescue, to save!

Two fish. Five loaves of bread. One Savior offers physical nourishment to thousands.

Three nails. Two pieces of wood. One Savior offers endless nourishment to a world dying of spiritual hunger:

Blessed are those who hunger and thirst for righteousness, for they shall be satisfied.
Matthew 5:6

In a crowd of 5,000 or a party of one, Jesus' awesome and miraculous powers are for all believers. There is no problem he can't solve. There is no hurt too big for his comfort. There is no sinner he doesn't love.

→ **PRAYER STARTER:** Jesus, I praise you for your endless nourishment . . .

Sharing the Memories

For God so loved the world, that he gave his only Son,
that whoever believes in him should not perish
but have eternal life.
John 3:16

I have fond childhood memories of my family gathering in my aunt and uncle's basement to share 16mm movies of their travels. Ask teenagers today about 16mm film and they'll laugh you out of the room!

Today's technology makes it possible to share our stories at any time, anywhere. You can broadcast live around the globe and share your pictures within seconds of capturing the moment.

We can share God's story with that same speed and unlimited audience. People across the ocean can see your worship service proclaiming the message of God's love and salvation through Jesus. Urgent prayer requests can fly through social media, reaching thousands of people in minutes. Everyone on Facebook, Twitter, and Instagram can see how Jesus' story has changed your story.

The potential for sharing God's Word through technology is almost unlimited, but it can't replace having a face-to-face conversation with someone who is missing out on the grace of Jesus.

It's easy to overlook these opportunities. We know Jesus. Prayer and worship are integral parts of our lives. But, for many, God's story is a fairy tale. The Good News Jesus brings is too good to be true.

A woman in my local foster-care community recently shared a heartbreaking story. She woke up on Sunday morning, following her usual routine of church and Bible study. That week, she took a child from foster care with her. When the two sat down in the pew, the little boy pointed to the crucifix on the altar and asked, "Who is that man on the wood?"

That man is Jesus—Savior, Friend, Light of the World.

You may be surprised to know how many people live their lives apart from Jesus. It's easy to think about the millions of people across the ocean who don't yet know Jesus. But, have you considered the people in your neighborhood, your children's school, and your social circle? Or your mail carrier, your boss, your running buddy?

Do they know Jesus? Do you care enough to share God's Word with them?

→ **PRAYER STARTER:** Forgive me, Jesus, when I neglect to share the Good News of Calvary's cross with those around me . . .

Traveling with Gratitude

*I give thanks to my God always for you because of the
grace of God that was given you in Christ Jesus*

1 Corinthians 1:4

Bickering is par for the course when you're traveling on
a family vacation. Kids become impatient, crabby, and
frustrated. Even adults can be overheard saying, "I can't
spend another minute in that car!"

For many of us, fighting, bickering, and anger combine
in a go-to response in trying situations. An attitude of
gratitude? Not so much. Do any of these sound familiar?

→ Loud sighs and obvious eye rolls while waiting in line at
   the post office
→ Complaints about your nonexistent raise at work
→ A "not my kid!" reaction to a phone call from your
   child's teacher

Gratitude doesn't come easy for us, and we're not the
only ones. Remember God's chosen people, Israel? They
grumbled when they found themselves just steps away
from the blessings of the
Promised Land (Numbers
14:1–4). The prodigal son in
his early days? A reckless,
greedy jerk (Luke 15:11–13).
The ten lepers healed by
Jesus? Only one
said thanks (Luke 17:11–19).

Even though our gratitude never matches the magnitude of our blessings, God keeps on giving. When we're at our worst—spiteful, and thinking we deserve more than we're getting—God is still there, pouring down his blessings like rain. He sent the ultimate blessing in his only Son, Jesus:

For while we were still weak, at the right time Christ died for the ungodly. For one will scarcely die for a righteous person . . . but God shows his love for us in that while we were still sinners, Christ died for us.

Romans 5:6–8

Though we are ungrateful, though we often display ugly attitudes, our Lord is always ready to forgive. In infinite love and mercy, Jesus covers us in his very own righteousness!

A million songs of praise would never be enough to express our gratitude for the gift of our Savior, but don't let that stop you! Thank your Travel Guide, Jesus—in every moment. Thank him for his grace, forgiveness, and salvation.

As the Holy Spirit cultivates an attitude of gratitude in your life, you'll discover easily overlooked blessings. Then, your thanksgiving will begin to multiply. Your gratitude will flow steadily to your Savior and spill over into responses of thanksgiving to those around you.

→ **PRAYER STARTER:** Holy Spirit, fill my heart with gratitude . . .

Almost Home

Our citizenship is in heaven, and from it we
await a Savior, the Lord Jesus Christ
Philippians 3:20

It's music to your ears! Hearing "We're almost home!" after a long road trip. It's comforting to know that you'll soon be out of the car and back in your house, your bed, and your normal routine.

The apostle Paul took comfort in two homes—his earthly ministry and his heavenly mansion. He shared these thoughts with God's people in Philippi:

Christ will be honored in my body, whether by life or by death. For to me to live is Christ, and to die is gain. . . . I am hard pressed between the two. My desire is to depart and be with Christ, for that is far better. But to remain in the flesh is more necessary on your account.

Philippians 1:20–24

Paul longed to be with Christ, but he also loved his calling here on earth. He had a passion to advance the Gospel so that more people could call heaven home. He lived confidently, knowing that if Christ returned before he died, his life would continue in his Savior's presence. And, if he died, he knew he would continue to live in that same presence in heaven.

For Paul and for us, eternal life doesn't start when we die or when Christ returns. We're living it now! By faith in Jesus, we are able to know God and experience the blessings of that relationship *right now.* Paul describes the promise of Scripture and our sure hope:

He who began a good work in [us] will bring it to completion at the day of Jesus Christ.

Philippians 1:6

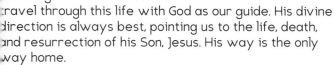

We can truly look forward to Christ's triumphant return and his gift of heaven as we travel through this life with God as our guide. His divine direction is always best, pointing us to the life, death, and resurrection of his Son, Jesus. His way is the only way home.

Yes, the best of our travels is yet to come. We're almost home. What a perfect ending, without an end!

→ **PRAYER STARTER:** Dear Lord, point me in the direction of Jesus, my Savior. I'm relying on your grace and presence as you lead me on this never-ending journey . . .

I lift up my eyes to the hills.
From where does my help come?
My help comes from the LORD,
who made heaven and earth. Psalm 121:1–2

This Scripture is commonly known as "The Travelers Psalm." Open your Bible and read the complete psalm, paying special attention to the great number of promises God makes to you there.

We're at the end of this devotional journey now, but your Guide will continue to travel with you always. Incorporate his Word and the topics from this week into your daily life. Find nourishment and rest in him, praise him for the blessing of eternal life, and proclaim his name throughout all your life's travels!

God's direction is always best. He has the entire journey already worked out, and he assures us that *all of it* will work for the good of his people. Best of all, Jesus and his promises follow you wherever you go. Forgiveness frees, lives change, faith grows, and hope triumphs for those who dwell in Jesus' presence.

To see all of CTA's devotion books and journals, visit us at www.CTAinc.com.

If this book has made a difference in your life or if you have simply enjoyed it, we would like to hear from you. Your words will encourage us!

→ E-mail: editor@CTAinc.com; include the subject line: GBD18SC

→ Write: Editorial Manager, Department
GBD18SC
CTA, Inc.
PO Box 1205
Fenton, MO 63026-1205

→ Comment online: www.CTAinc.com (search GBD18SC)

Splat the Cat

The Big Helper

Based on the bestselling books by Rob Scotton
Cover art by Rick Farley
Text by J. E. Bright
Illustrations by Loryn Brantz

HARPER
An Imprint of HarperCollinsPublishers

© 2020 CFA Properties, Inc. Chick-fil-A® and the Chick-fil-A Kids Logo™ are
trademarks of CFA Properties, Inc. www.chick-fil-a.com Chick-fil-A, Inc., Atlanta, GA 30349
Adapted from the original for Chick-fil-A, Inc. by Frederic Thomas USA, Inc.
Made in USA, Frederic Thomas, USA, Inc., 10/2019 Splat the Cat - The Big Helper

"Family meeting!" Splat's father called from upstairs.

"We're a very busy family," Dad said. "We all need to pitch in.
So I've made a list of daily to-dos for you to check off each day."

"A to-do list?" said Splat. He had a bad feeling about this.

Splat's jobs were to make his bed, put away his toys, and water the plants.
"But . . . ," Splat sputtered. "That'll take forever!"
"If you do your little part," said Dad, "it'll be a big help."

Splat and Seymour went back to playing their game.
After a half hour, Seymour pointed to the to-do list.
"We can do them later," Splat replied.

Splat's
Daily To-Do
☐ Make bed
☐ Put toys away
☐ Water plants

"New rule," Mom declared. "No television or video games until everything is checked off your list."

"Awwww," Splat moaned.

Splat went to his room. It was a total mess. "Let's get this over with so we can get back to our game, Seymour!" he said.

Splat made his bed.

He put away his toys.

SPLASH!

Then he watered his plant. . . .

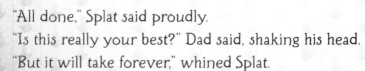

"All done," Splat said proudly.
"Is this really your best?" Dad said, shaking his head.
"But it will take forever," whined Splat.

"You know how they say that time flies when you're having fun?" Splat's dad said. Splat nodded. He sure did. "So . . . make it fun."

Splat decided to try.

This time when Splat made his bed, he imagined he was fishing in the ocean.

His pillow turned into a giant shark, and everything else on the floor became a different fish or sea creature.

When he cleaned up his toys, Splat imagined that he was a pirate! Each toy was a jewel or gold coin—and his toy box was a treasure chest.

When he watered his plant, he pretended he was a jungle explorer.

"All done!" said Splat.

"Great job, Splat," Splat's dad said.
"Now you can play your video game," added his mom.

As Splat sat down to play his video game, he noticed a few things that needed to be put away.

"I'll be right back, Seymour," he said. "I've got to go on a quick arctic expedition."

He never imagined helping out could be so much fun.